MUSIC: OUR UNIVERSAL LANGUAGE

MUSIC
OUR UNIVERSAL LANGUAGE

A Singer's First Step to Fluency

GERALD WHITE

Music 1on1 Publishing

LOS ANGELES

Music 1 on 1 Publishing

Copyright © 2009 by Gerald White

All rights reserved. Printed in the United States of America. No part of this book may be reproduced in any manner whatsoever without written permission except in the case of brief quotations embodied in critical articles and reviews.

For information about special sales, bulk purchases, or to contact Gerald, contact www.music1on1.com.

Cover design by: Cris Kallestad
Layout and editing by Memoirs Ink. (www.memoirsink.com)

Library of Congress Cataloging-in-Publication Data

White, Gerald
Music: Our Universal Language; A Singer's First Step to Fluency

p. cm.
1. Sightsinging—Music Theory—Singing—Vocal Practice

ISBN: 978-0-578-02483-7

*I would like to dedicate
this book to my music teacher for 10 years,
Dr. Ralph Taylor.*

Table of Contents

1. **LEARN TO READ MUSIC THROUGH SINGING** 12
   - Exceptions 14
2. **THE NUMBER 7** 16
3. **7 LETTERS** 17
   - The 8 Note Scale 21
   - Singing the Scale 22
   - 7 Notes and Rests 23
   - Note Breakdown 25
4. **7 TIME SIGNATURES** 26
5. **7 SHARP AND FLAT KEYS** 30
   - Determining Key Signatures 31
   - Key Signatures Other Than C 32
   - Key Chart 33
   - Application 34
6. **7 SYMBOLS** 35
   - Additional Terms 36
7. **7 DYNAMICS** 37
8. **IN A NUT SHELL** 38
   - Altered Notes Not Belonging to the Scale 40
9. **MUSCLE MEMORY** 41
10. **INTERVALS** 42
    - Examples of Intervals 43
    - Inverted Intervals 45
11. **THINGS TO THINK ABOUT** 46
12. **IN CLOSING** 48

Introduction

LEARNING THE CRAFT FROM A MASTER
by Lauri D. Goldenhersh

LOS ANGELES—A couple of weeks ago, I had the pleasure of sitting in on two of the three SAG/AFTRA sightsinging courses taught by Gerald White. Gerald is one of the most sought-after session singers in town, which says a lot, since those lists seem to get shorter by the minute. I've heard about him over and over during the past few years, and was honored when he agreed to let me come and observe, so that I could report to all of you.

What immediately impressed me was the diversity of focus in his student groups: in both the intermediate and advanced classes (I attended one of each), there were singers of classical, jazz, R&B, pop/rock, sacred and country music. The ranks included several Lauri's List members (go team!) and even a few members of the LA Master Chorale, even though that designation is generally used as an "oh, yeah, you can read" barometer in and of itself. (Bravo! to those singers for exerting the effort to keep those chops up, as we all must.) There were active session singers and hopefuls, and plenty of really good amateurs, particularly from two community choirs I know, improving their skills to broaden their horizons. They won't be amateurs for long—we should all be so smart.

What everyone had in common was their commitment: they were there to do real work and gain real skills. Any air of competition or ego was short-lived, as White's approach is generally focused on the work, and leaves little room for one-upsmanship or showing off. In an atmosphere of support and goal-driven cooperation, he gets down to business and stays on task. (As we know, that, in itself, is a near-miracle.) So much concept and so many lightning-fast exercises were consumed in the advanced class that it left even one of the LAMC members crying, "my brain hurts!" But they continued, got over the bump, and everyone learned a lot.

WHY WE NEED THIS

The reality is that many otherwise competent vocalists need time and help in building their sightreading proficiency, even after graduating from prestigious university and conservatory programs. But countless independent sightsinging courses (i.e. those offered outside a formal school curriculum) are far too elementary or unstructured, designed to be either an introduction to reading for the complete novice, or a series of general practice sessions with little structure and no end in sight. In fact, some are very clearly conceived to provide ongoing income for the instructor, and are justified, lamely, as a vague and mysterious process which "cannot be explained, only experienced," or some such nonsense. (Sheesh!)

Reading music and sightreading are, for the most part, finite skills. They involve ongoing practice, as does any language study, but some level of fluency is an attainable goal for most people, so cloaking the process in mystery builds nothing but the instructor's stock portfolio. A lack of conceptual substance may be proffered as Zen or as some sort of organic learning process, but without an understanding of the theory behind the music on the page, practice isn't enough. The combination is key, or singers will have a tough time applying the work in rehearsal. The good news is that the theory required is quite simple. It just needs a good teacher to get the point across.

LIFTING THE VEIL

Theoretically, White is doing what some other teachers already do: he's teaching Movable Doh, but with numbers instead of solfege syllables. He uses acknowledged tools and time-honored methods: transcription, dictation, scales, repetition, and cold reading from old and new sightreading resources. But he makes it practical, throwing his singers into the pool with an extensive library of real-life session charts, teaching them what to expect and how to approach it in the day-to-day. He has a gift for teaching within the familiar, dispensing with the need for constant translation when new challenges arise. (e.g. Do-re-mi is a new language for some, while 1-2-3 is not.) Ultimately, he gives his students simple tools they can embrace quickly and carry with them for the rest of their lives.

For instance, White takes the time to make clear and logical sense of the physical disconnect between the way singers and instrumentalists experience scales. Since many singers were taught sightreading by instrumentalists in the first place, this lesson is invaluable. A flute player, for example, learns scales by memorizing specific, targeted physical motions (press this key, then these...) depending on the key signature. Since singers have no keys to press, sounding the pitches may seem like a more uncertain endeavor. They may feel entirely dependent on reference pitches and sensory memory, which is a very quick road to "I'm a no-talent hack." Many singers find themselves disgruntled and frustrated by this process, and simply give up. But with an easy understanding of how individual pitches work within the scale, those same singers find their way around the page, and are less flummoxed by key changes or accidentals. In time, they become flexible and intuitive musicians.

White also speaks very effectively on pitfalls like "musical autopilot," where singers may depart from the score because they "know" what's coming, or to do their own thing. But instead of harsh warnings to stay on the page or complicated theories on how to outthink the impulse, he offers practical examples of how things work in professional situations. He helps his students practice how to stay focused, keep going, even how to pick up again when they get lost.

This no-nonsense approach cuts through the sometimes cryptic fog of theory, breaking down those elusive but essential principles to the bare bones of what singers need to know, and it empowers them to own the knowledge and take responsibility for their own skill-building. They find they can work easily and continually on their own, because they now know just what to do, and they can do much of it anywhere. A homework assignment of transcribing a TV theme, for instance, kick-starts the habit of thinking about visual notation when they hear any tune—he's encouraging them to apply it to daily life, not just their musical activities. His scale exercises are simple, direct and easy to remember, but they're also fun—musical puzzles you can launch into anywhere, and you'll want to. Some students report that they find themselves practicing all the time, even unconsciously, and their newfound knowledge becomes a built-in part of their lives. It's as if they're in a language immersion program, and they're finding chances to "speak" music everywhere they go.

This article was originally published at www.LaurisList.com.

1 | LEARN TO READ MUSIC THROUGH SINGING

Are you someone who has been on the world's largest stage but doesn't know what key you are singing in?

Are you a community or church choir member who holds the music with a blank stare, hoping the person next to you sings loud enough so you can learn your part?

Do you hope that your agent sends you a copy of the music via CD or MP3 the night before so you can cram it all in overnight for your audition?

In music class, does the thought of your teacher calling on you frighten you to death?

Are you the person who sings higher when the notes go up and lower when they go down, hoping you've guessed the correct pitch?

IF YOU ANSWERED YES TO ANY OR ALL OF THESE QUESTIONS, THEN YOU ARE IN THE RIGHT PLACE AND YOU SHOULD KNOW THAT YOU ARE NOT ALONE.

As I write this, I'm thinking of how many books are out there about theory. So what is different about this one?

Through my 25 years of teaching music theory, I've seen that the biggest obstacle for people learning to read music is *too much information*. If you take a theory class in college, you'll study everything from modes to 12 tone serialism. That's not a bad thing—it's just not what you need to know when learning the basics of music and how it works.

Over the years, I was shocked at how many people in my classes had toured the world stages, had wonderful careers as musicians and singers, and a few even had music degrees, yet they did not understand music, did not know their key signatures, or could not sing a simple melody written on paper. My goal became to figure out why this was happening and to try to bridge the gap so that your understanding of this universal language can be a simple process. That's how this book originated.

Being a musician and not understanding music is no different than someone who lives in Mexico for 20 years and still can't speak Spanish. I encourage you to take the time to go through a few simple steps so that you can understand and utilize this beautiful language. Music is so powerful. It's one of the few things in life that stimulates both sides of the brain at the same time, as well as our emotions and senses.

Most everyone who learns music learns with an instrument, like piano or guitar. But if you don't play an instrument, you may sit in theory class with no way to apply what you are learning. I say, use your built in instrument—your voice.

The difference between using your voice and an instrument like piano or guitar is that you are training your vocal cords to adjust to form pitches. The actual notes on a piano or guitar never change. But because your cords are made of flesh and blood, it's a bit more challenging to train your cords to respond correctly, yet once you master a few elements, the process in the long run is quite simple.

I was never a great sight reader. In fact, it was hard for me to learn to read because I relied on my ear and was often disgusted at the thought of practicing music theory. My instructor in college would play a Chopin piece and as long as I could hear it, I could play it. He quickly figured me out and stopped playing it. I then was faced with begrudgingly and painstakingly going note by note to figure out how to play Chopin. It wasn't until after I completed my degree and began a career which required proficient reading, that I broke the process down to a few simple rules that worked for me.

Learning to read music through singing will allow you to look at a piece of music and sing it without help from anyone. An official term often used for this process is **sightsinging**. It's another language. It's universal and it's beautiful. So, let's get started.

Exceptions

Just for disclaimer purposes, let me get one thing out of the way. There are always exceptions to everything I will say in this book. Music is not absolute.

Webster's Dictionary defines music as: "...any agreeable sound." This has always been funny to me. If we agree that it's music, then so be it. And, if we agree that this will work in a very simplified form, it will. So when I state there are 7 different kinds of notes, it literally means that for the purpose of this book and your ability to comprehend the basics of music, there are 7 different kinds of notes. How many are there really? An infinite number.

To illustrate my point, let's say you have a chocolate pie and that pie will be shared with your guests. You could have one large piece for yourself or if you cut the pie in half, there are then two pieces. Cut it once more and you have quarter pieces and so on. If you keep cutting, you could technically create hundreds of pieces of that pie. But into how many pieces do you normally cut a pie so that your guests will enjoy it and will want to visit again? Probably about 8 or so.

> *Webster's Dictionary defines music as: "...any agreeable sound." This has always been funny to me. If we agree that it's music, then so be it.*

Notes can be thought of in the same way. They represent an amount of time and every time you cut the value of a note in half, it becomes twice as fast and could technically become hundreds of different kinds of notes. For our purposes, there are 7 most commonly used notes. To make this entire process easy to understand and get your hands on, I will give you the most common forms of all aspects of music and give you an absolute with which to work. Got it?

By the way, this book is for those whom the light has not yet come on when it comes to understanding music. You may be from any musical background or level but something is still missing. If you are advanced and looking for exercises to keep your chops up and expand your knowledge, stay tuned. That book is on its way. I have quite an array of workouts that will put you to the test.

My goal in this book is for you to understand how music notation works. You will grasp the concept and be able to work your way into sightreading.

2 | THE NUMBER 7

I always think of 7 as a lucky number. There are 7 colors in the rainbow, 7 chakras in the human body, 7 days in our week, etc. Music is very mathematical. For those of you like me who didn't do well in Math, don't worry. It all fits together like a puzzle and is made of 7 simple aspects:

7 NOTES (LETTERS)
7 RHYTHMICAL NOTES AND RESTS
7 TIME SIGNATURES
7 SHARP KEYS
7 FLAT KEYS
7 BASIC SYMBOLS
7 DYNAMICS

It's really that easy. The hard part is processing speed. How fast can you put the elements to work? This will be determined by how much time you spend practicing what you learn.

3 | 7 LETTERS

What are the 7 letters used in music?

A, B, C, D, E, F, and G—each representing a different pitch.

Is that all? Yes. These are the only ones. These 7 letters are used to give a name to the different pitches that we experience. Because there are 12 pitches total, we add other words/symbols to these 7 letters to encompass all 12 pitches, such as A flat (b), or F sharp (#).

There are 3 words used to alter these music letters. These words are:

FLAT represented by the symbol (♭). When this symbol is present, the note written is lowered by one half step.

SHARP represented by the symbol (♯). When this symbol is present, the note written is raised by one half step.

NATURAL represented by the symbol (♮). When this symbol is present, the note written is altered back to its original pitch after being sharp or flat.

I've mentioned the terms **half step** and **whole step**. A half step is a move of 1 note in either direction. A whole step is a move of 2 notes in either direction. The only use of half and whole steps will be in regards to the raised note symbol (♯) or the lowered note symbol (♭).

For the purposes of simplicity, I'm going to instruct based on scale placement by numbers instead of half and whole steps.

For Example:

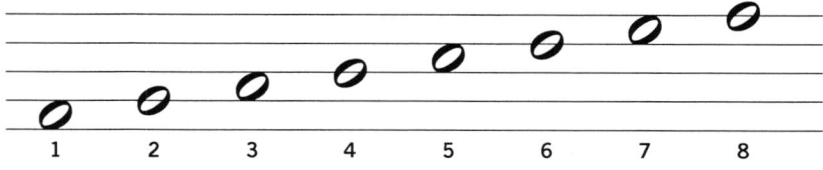

Each of the 7 letters will be represented by a number.
These 7 letters mentioned above are placed on a grid called a **stave**.

It looks like this:

Two staves are combined to form a **staff**. The staff is the grid where all of our notes are placed.

It looks like this:

The symbol 𝄞 is called a treble clef. It represents the area most commonly used for high voices or high pitched instruments.

The symbol 𝄢 is called a bass clef. It represents the area most commonly used for low voices or low pitched instruments.

There is a space in the middle of the two staves which is left open for lyrics, although there is an invisible line in the middle where the note Middle C is located.

We use only 5 lines in each section because as stated, it's these areas that contain the most common pitches we hear. If all notes were included, the lines would be continuous in both directions looking like this:

Sometimes notes are written above or below the staff in cases where we need extremely high pitches or extremely low pitches. When this occurs, these notes are written on small lines called ledger lines and are added as needed. They look like this:

Our 7 letters, each representing a different note, are placed on these lines and spaces as follows:

C
D
E
F
G
A
B
C
D
E
F
B
A
G
F
E
D
C
B
A
G

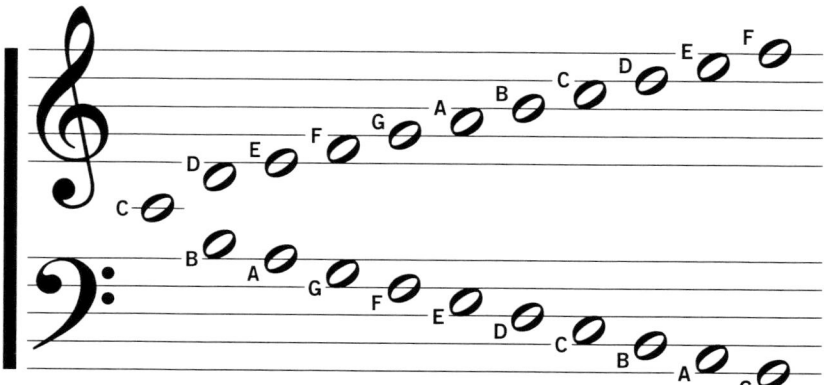

If you will notice, the letters are placed in ascending order from bottom to top. Once you get to the letter G in the alphabet, you start over again with the letter A.

There are acronyms used by many to learn where these letters (notes) are placed. Such as F, A, C, E, which shows the letters in the spaces of the treble clef. The best way, however, is to memorize where these notes are.

If you are reading ascending pitches, you move forward in the alphabet. A, B, C, D, E, F, and G, which causes you to produce higher pitches.

If you are reading descending pitches, you move backwards in the alphabet. G, F, E, D, C, B, and A, which causes you to produce lower pitches.

Each letter will be given a number. Since there are 7 letters, there are 7 numbers used to represent these letters. These letters (in order) form what we call an 8 note scale. The 8th note is a repeat of the first note.

The 8 Note Scale

The 8 note scale is what we base all of our music on. I recommend stopping at this point and learning this 8 note scale. You can start on any pitch. Have someone play this scale for you and memorize it like you would a song.

Find a pitch to start your scale that easily fits your range and sing it over and over with the numbers 1-8. The chart on the following page is a great tool in practicing the scale and getting it engrained into your system.

> *...in my 25 years of music, whether in film, TV, live, in class or in the studio, I've never been asked to sing "fi" or "re" by a director or producer.*

Before we continue, here is a note about **solfeggio** (do, re, mi, etc). I grew up learning solfeggio which is a system of names given to the different pitches. There is nothing wrong with this system. It works, but I have found that understanding number placement is a much easier process for most people. Also, in my 25 years of music, whether in film, TV, live, in class or in the studio, I've never been asked to sing "fi" or "re" by a director or producer.

Singing The Scale

Start by singing a scale using the numbers 1-8.
You can hear this scale from a friend who knows how to play.

1–2–3–4–5–6–7–8–7–6–5–4–3–2–1
1–2–3–4–5–6–7–8–7–6–5–4–3–2–1

Now sing the scale by adding a new number as you go.

1
1–2–1
1–2–3–2–1
1–2–3–4–3–2–1
1–2–3–4–5–4–3–2–1
1–2–3–4–5–6–5–4–3–2–1
1–2–3–4–5–6–7–6–5–4–3–2–1
1–2–3–4–5–6–7–8–7–6–5–4–3–2–1
8
8–7–8
8–7–6–7–8
8–7–6–5–6–7–8
8–7–6–5–4–5–6–7–8
8–7–6–5–4–3–4–5–6–7–8
8–7–6–5–4–3–2–3–4–5–6–7–8
8–7–6–5–4–3–2–1–2–3–4–5–6–7–8

Now you may try this exercise by leaving out one number.
Make sure you also leave out the appropriate pitch.
Try leaving out the number 3 as shown below.

1
1–2–1
1–2–__–2–1
1–2–__–4–__–2–1

7 NOTES & RESTS

Once you learn where the pitches are located on the staff and you can sing your major scale from any of those pitches, it's important to know how long to hold each pitch. That length of time is determined by 7 note symbols and 7 rest symbols. Each note symbol represents an amount of time a pitch is played or sung. Each rest symbol represents an amount of time that you are to remain quiet. Sometimes I think we need more rest symbols. ☻

When you see a symbol that represents an allotted amount of time, you will sing a note and hold it for a certain number of counts, or you will remain quiet for a certain number of counts.

Each rest symbol represents an amount of time that you are to remain quiet. Sometimes I think we need more rest symbols.

Below is a list of 7 note symbols, 7 rest symbols and how much time they each represent.

1	𝅝	Whole Note: 4 counts
	▬	Whole Rest: 4 counts
2	𝅗𝅥.	Dotted Half Note: 3 counts
	▬ 𝄾	Dotted Half Rest: 3 counts (more common than ▬·)
3	𝅗𝅥	Half Note: 2 counts
	▬	Half Rest: 2 counts
4	𝅘𝅥.	Dotted Quarter Note: 1 ½ counts
	𝄽 𝄾	Dotted Quarter Rest: 1 ½ counts (more common than 𝄽·)
5	𝅘𝅥	Quarter Note: 1 count
	𝄽	Quarter Rest: 1 count
6	𝅘𝅥𝅮	Eight Note: ½ count
	𝄾	Eight Rest: ½ count
7	𝅘𝅥𝅯	Sixteenth Note: ¼ count
	𝄿	Sixteenth Rest: ¼ count

Note Breakdown

If you were to start with the longest note and break it down to the smallest, this chart shows what that would look like.

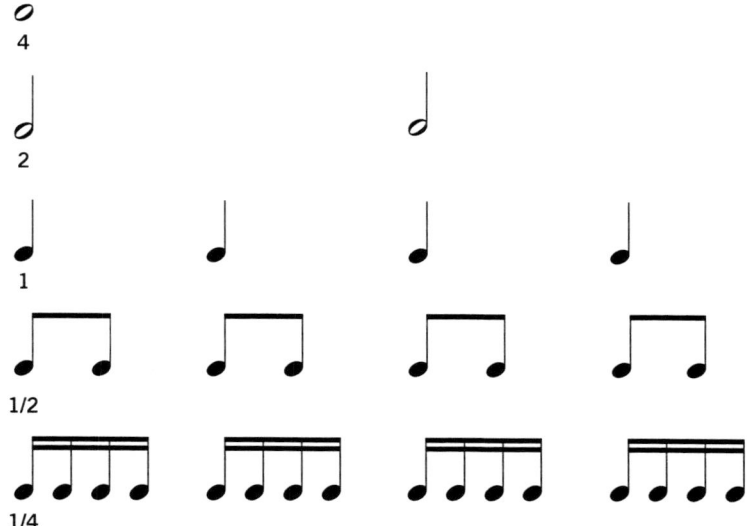

Here are a few more examples of note values regarding time:

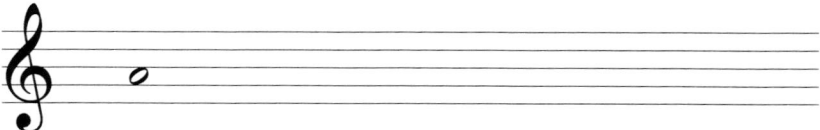

The note above is an A. It's also a whole note symbol so you would sing the A and hold it for 4 counts.

These notes are on the B line. They are half note symbols so you would sing a B and hold it for 2 counts, and sing another B and hold it for 2 counts.

4 | 7 TIME SIGNATURES

In all noted music, there are **measures.** These are blocks of the musical staff that separate the music into sections. Each section will contain the same amount of counts once the time signature is determined. The measures look like this:

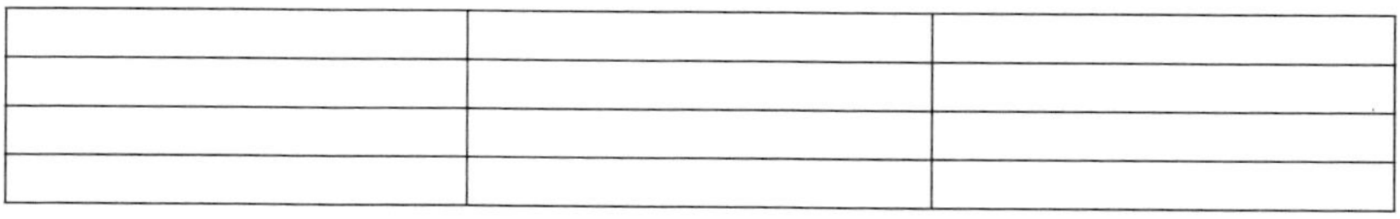

If the music has $\frac{4}{4}$ written in the beginning, that simply means that every measure in that song will have 4 beats. The bottom number states which kind of note the beat falls on—in this case the quarter note (♩), because there is a four on the bottom of the fraction.

In $\frac{3}{4}$ time, there is a value of 3 quarter notes (♩) in each measure and the quarter note gets the beat.

In $\frac{6}{8}$ time, there is a value of 6 eighth notes (♪) in each measure and the eighth note gets the beat.

And so on.

The 7 most common time signatures are: $\frac{2}{2}$ $\frac{2}{4}$ $\frac{3}{4}$ $\frac{4}{4}$ $\frac{6}{8}$ $\frac{9}{8}$ $\frac{12}{8}$

Think of the beat as a metronome or bass drum that is steady and never changes. The rhythms change but the beats don't change. They are steady and hold the music together in a set time signature.

Simply put, if the fraction is 4/4, then you have the value of 4 quarter notes in each measure. If the fraction is 3/4, then you have the value of 3 quarter notes in each measure. If the fraction is 6/8, then you have the value of 6 eighth notes in each measure.

See if you can come up with examples of the different time signatures and then clap them. Make sure you add up the note values in each measure to come up with the correct number of beats. Use combinations from the 7 note symbols and 7 rests symbols on page 24.

Look at the example below. In each line, there is one measure which is incorrect. See if you can find which measure that is.

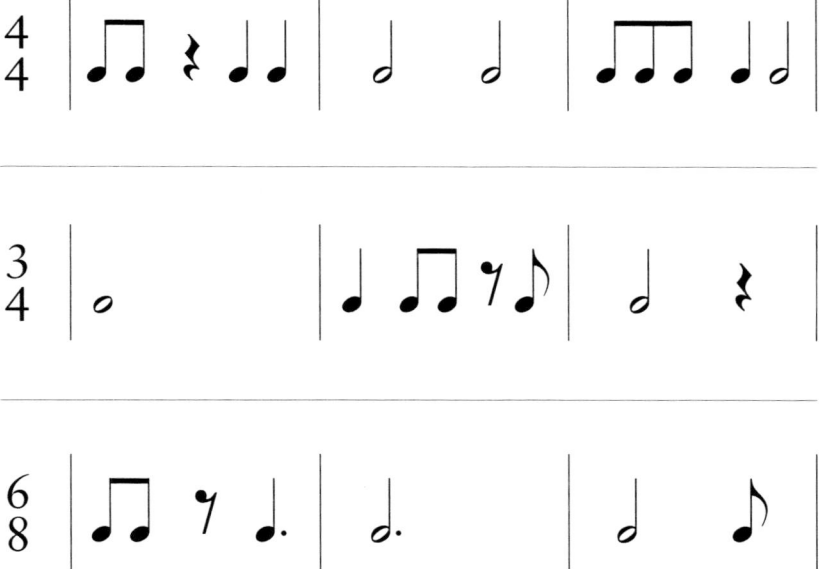

When you first start learning to clap rhythms, it's best to place numbers where each new note starts in the measure. Each division of a beat has a name which is illustrated below.

In this example of 4/4 time, you count the quarter note as the beat.
- The first symbol is a quarter note that starts on beat 1 and lasts for 1 count.
- The second symbol is a rest that starts on beat 2 and lasts for 1 count.
- The third symbol is an eighth note that starts on beat 3 and lasts for ½ count.
- The fourth symbol is an eighth note that starts on the second half of beat 3 and lasts for ½ count.
- The fifth symbol is a quarter note that starts on beat 4 and lasts for 1 count.

Always place numbers where the note starts and not where the rest starts. Notice that there is a slash for every quarter of a beat. This is the smallest division and will help you understand where the beats are landing.

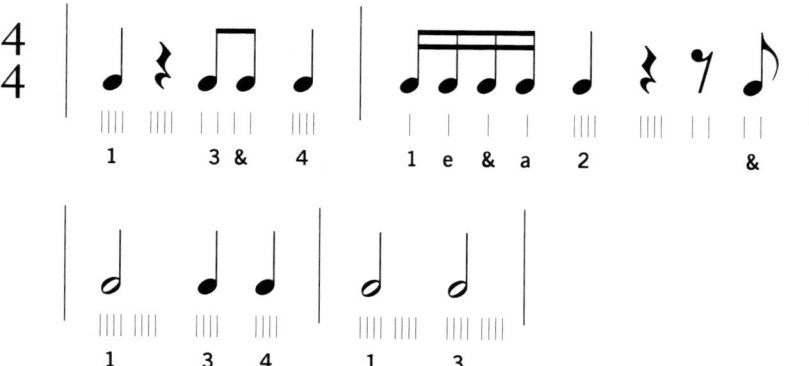

Notice that the two eighth notes are beamed together. ♪♪

It's much easier to read than when they are not beamed. ♪ ♪

In the next example of 6/8 time you count the eighth note as the beat:
- In the second measure, the first symbol is a dotted quarter note that starts on beat 1 and lasts for 3 beats. Why 3 beats and not 1 ½ beats? Because remember now we are in 6/8 time and we count the eighth notes as one beat each.
- The second symbol is a quarter rest that starts on beat 4 and lasts for 2 counts.
- The third symbol is an eighth note that starts on beat 6 and lasts for 1 count.

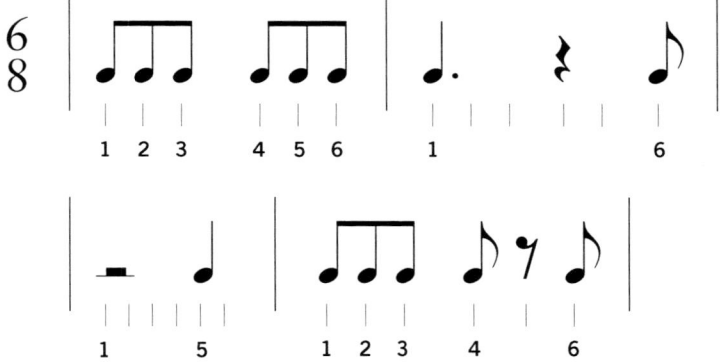

5 | 7 SHARP AND FLAT KEYS

Now we are at the most important section of this book. There is no question that the keys are *the key* to learning music and learning it well. If you are going to spend time on any of this process more than any other part, place your time here. Memorize the keys. Sleep on them. Study them until you know them like the back of your hand.

KEY	NO. OF SHARPS	KEY	KEY	NO. OF FLATS
G	1		F	1
D	2		B♭	2
A	3		E♭	3
E	4		A♭	4
B	5		D♭	5
F♯	6		G♭	6
C♯	7	C 0	C♭	7

If you will notice, most sharp keys don't have the sharp symbol beside them except for F# and C#. Most flat keys have the flat symbols beside them except for F. I have drawn a line between the two F's to show that F is the odd letter.

An important point to remember is that a letter's subsequent key always adds up to 7. For example, the key of G has 1 sharp. Gb has 6 flats. D has 2 sharps and Db has 5 flats, etc.

Also know that the letter C is the only letter that has 3 keys to its name. C, Cb and C#. Cb having 7 flats and C# having 7 sharps. All other letters have only two keys to their name.

Determining Key Signatures

I'll share several ways to determine which key the signature represents. The best way is to memorize them as listed on the following page, but you can look ahead to the Sightsinging Key Chart and follow a method I've come up with that is easy to learn and always dependable. It's based on the circle of 5ths. I will not go into that in this book, but know that because music is mathematical, this circle or chart will help you stay on track with your key signatures. It will also show how many sharps and flats are in each key.

Key Signatures Other Than C

G
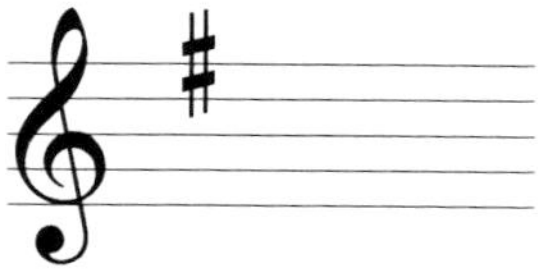

D
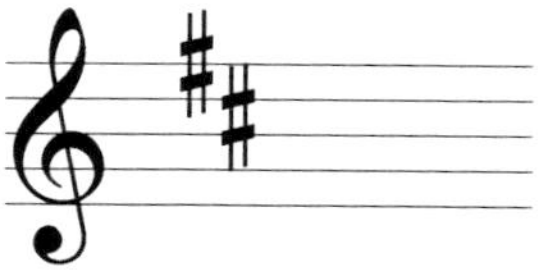

A
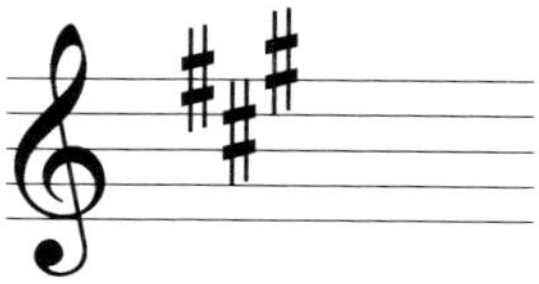

E
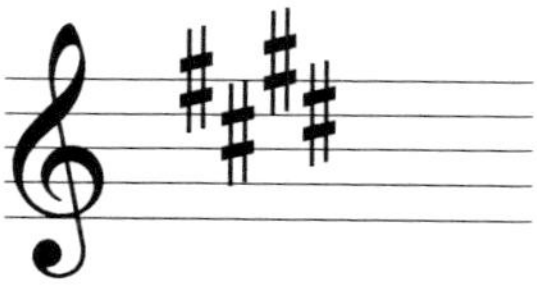

B
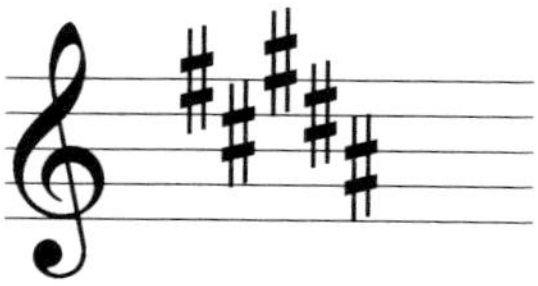

F#
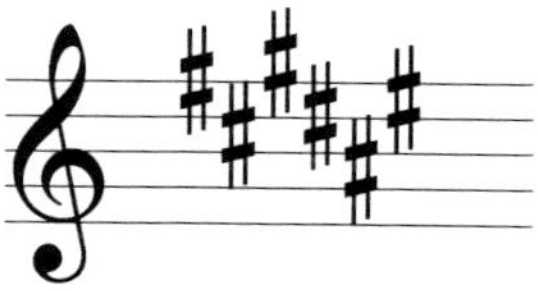

C#
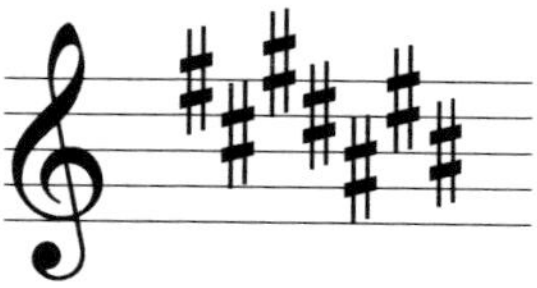

F
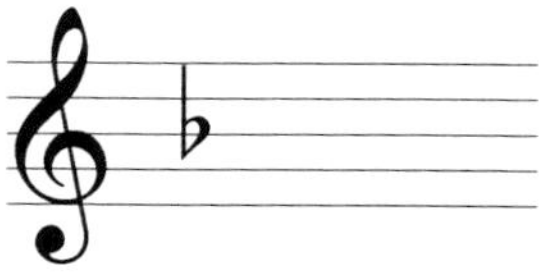

Bb
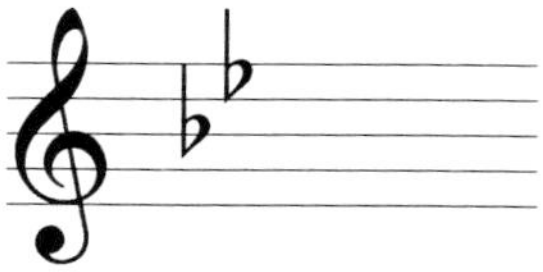

Eb
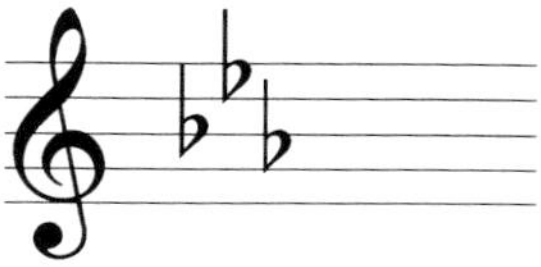

Ab
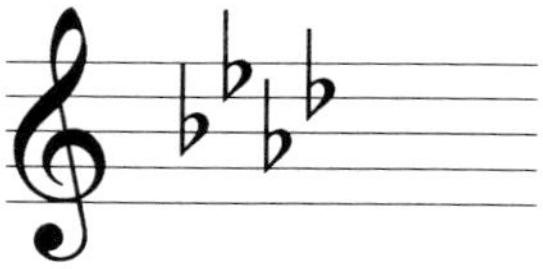

Db
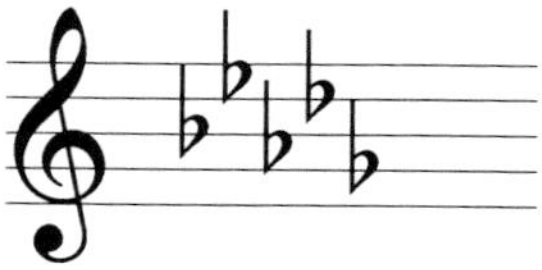

Gb
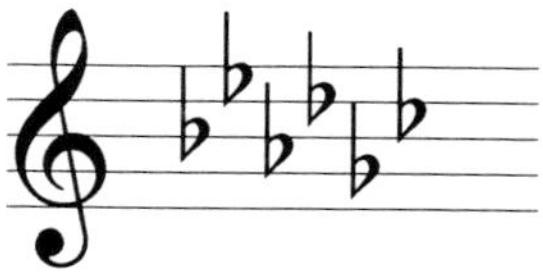

Cb
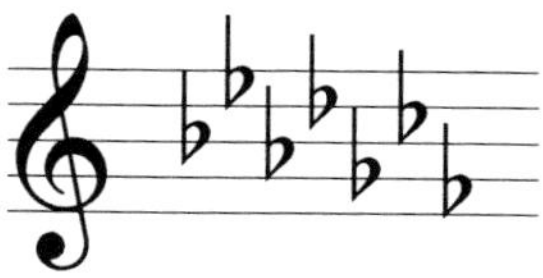

Key Chart for Determining Key Signatures

You will need to memorize this chart.
Come up with an acronym that works for you.

SHARPS

BEADGCF

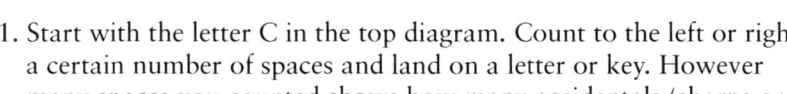

Remember that sharp keys are counted from right to left
and flat keys are counted from left to right.

FLATS

BEADGCF

1. Start with the letter C in the top diagram. Count to the left or right a certain number of spaces and land on a letter or key. However many spaces you counted shows how many accidentals (sharps or flats) are in that key.

2. Once you have established how many sharps or flats there are, start counting that many letters from the end of the row, and there you will have the accidentals present in the determined key.

3. For example, if you start on C and count to the left 3 spaces, you land on A. This tells you that A has 3 sharps. Why sharps? Because you counted from right to left. Since you counted 3 spaces, take that same number and count that many letters from the end. So F, C and G are the accidentals in the key of A.

Notice on the previous page that all accidentals (sharps and flats) are listed on the staff in a certain order. They must always follow this order and placement.

Application

These key signatures are basically codes that tell you where the keys start and end. Once you determine the code, you can start from 1 or (home) and sing every note in relation to the position of 1. At that point, you don't have to keep up with flats, sharps etc., because once you learn the eight note scale, it will be the same in each key. This is the beauty of using your voice rather than an instrument. Once you learn the scale with your voice it's the same process wherever you start. With an instrument, the notes are different colors, different shapes, different fingerings, etc.

The tones will start and end in a different place but the audible sequence is the same. For instance, the following example is in the key of D. So, the note D, which is the space below the bottom line in the treble clef and the 4th line up from the bottom (represented by the x below), is 1. The other notes will be sung in relation to 1. If you go up, you will increase in number and go higher in pitch. If you sing down, you will decrease in number and go lower in pitch.

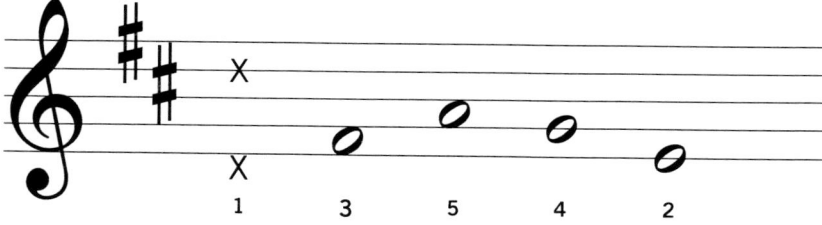

6 | 7 SYMBOLS

These symbols are common and will be used frequently in music.

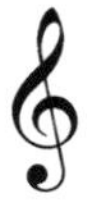

TREBLE CLEF
Symbol that represents an area where higher pitches occur.

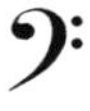

BASS CLEF
Symbol that represents an area where lower pitches occur.

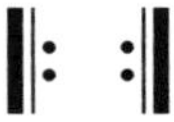

REPEAT SIGN This tells the reader to go back and sing the previous section over again.

D.S. This symbol is also a repeat symbol normally leading to the coda.

CODA
Symbol representing the end section of a piece of music.

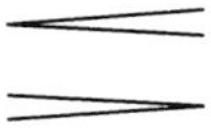

CRESCENDO AND DECRESCENDO
Gradually getting louder of softer.

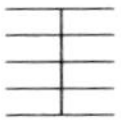

BAR LINE
Shows the starting and ending points of measure.

Additional Terms
Ties, Slurs, Triplets, Dotted Notes

TIE Curved line that joins two or more notes together without reemphasizing the second note. These notes stay the same.
Example below.

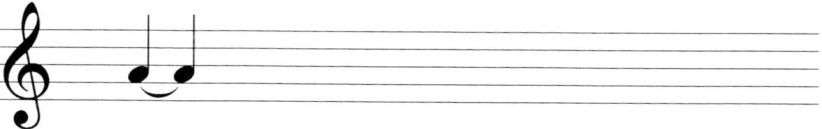

SLUR Curved line that joins two or more notes together where the notes change. This allows for smoother melodic movement without a breath and no attack of the second note. Example below.

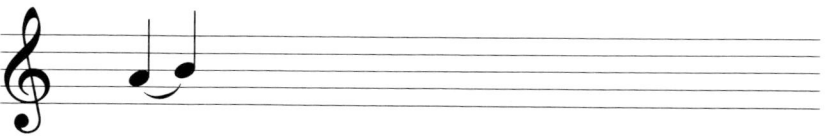

TRIPLETS Notes in groups of 3 that usually fill a space of 1, 2 or 4 counts creating a different mathematical and rhythmical structure. To fill a space of 1, 2 or 4 counts with 3 notes, select a note that represents half the amount of time of the determined space, and place 3 of those notes in succession with a beam across them. Add a bracket by the note heads and place the number 3 in the middle. To place 3 notes in the place of a half note (or 2 counts), do the following:

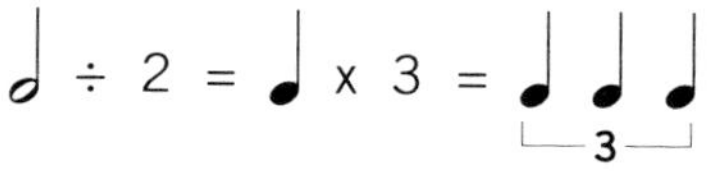

♩ ÷ 2 = ♩ x 3 = ♩♩♩
                   3

DOTTED NOTES - A dot next to a note adds half of the note's value to itself. For example, a quarter note with a dot makes the length of the note, 1½ beats.

♩ + ♪ = ♩.

1 + ½ = 1½

7 | 7 DYNAMICS

Last but certainly not least are the 7 dynamics of music. This represents volume levels and is crucial in giving movement and emotion to a song. I would venture to say that this one element is missing in most of today's music. Everything we hear is compressed to one level—loud.

1		Complete silence. Ah! Doesn't that sound wonderful?
2	*pp*	Pianissimo (very soft)
3	*p*	Piano (soft)
4	*mp*	Mezzo Piano (medium soft)
5	*mf*	Mezzo Forte (medium loud)
6	*f*	Forte (loud)
7	*ff*	Fortissimo (very loud)

8 | IN A NUTSHELL

Let's put all of the 7 steps together that we've learned and see how this works. I will walk you through the example below one step at a time.

1. Determine the key. The key is G because there is 1 sharp in the key signature.

2. Find the note G on the staff. This is symbolized below by the x on the second line.

3. Play the note G or have someone give you that pitch. The note G is now your home base for this particular song. It is also the 1st note of the key.

4. Determine the time signature. In this case, it's 4/4. This means that there is a value of 4 quarter notes in every measure and the beats occur on each quarter note value.

5. Now start with G and count up to the first note on the staff. Since you counted up 3 steps from G, the first note of your song is the third note of the major scale. Every note in a song is a number distance from the key represented in the key signature.

6. Remember that after you decide which key you are in and where your key center or home base is, then everything from there is a number relation to that starting point.

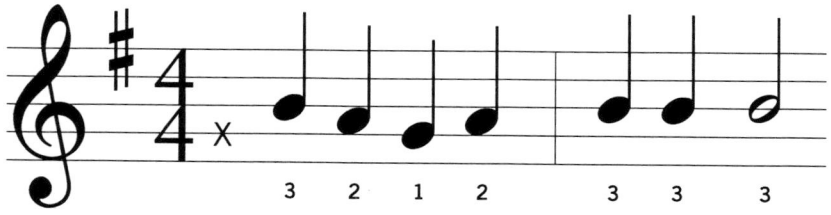

In the next three examples, the X signifies the key center and where 1 is located. Then the notes are sung in relation to that starting point.

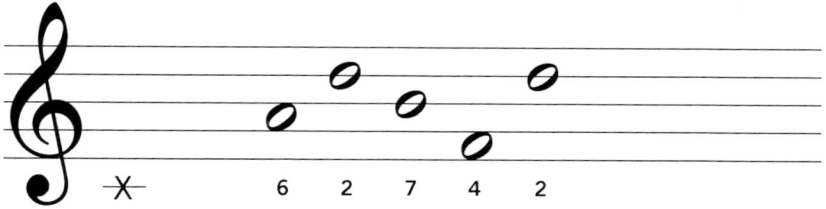

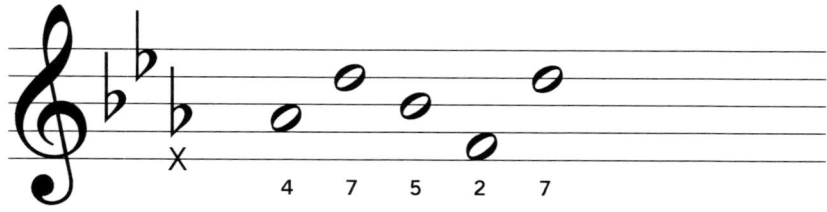

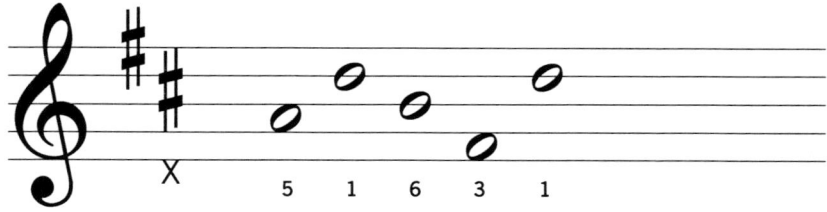

Altered Notes Not Belonging to the Scale

If you find an accidental within the music, it means that the note is altered and doesn't belong to the key or the scale you are singing. At this point, you must adjust your pitch a half step (up or down) in the direction of the accidental.

For instance, if you see a sharp, you are to raise the pitch by one half step. If you see a flat, you are to lower the pitch by one half step.

See example below.

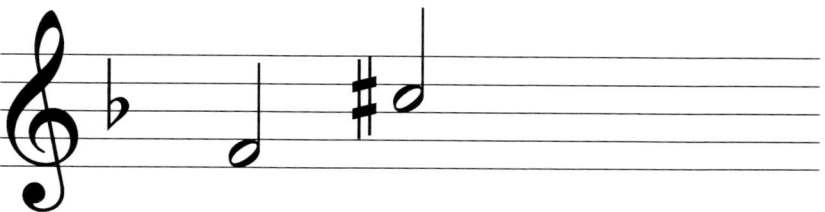

Notice that the second note (the 5 of the key), has a sharp by it. If you are singing from 1 to 5 and the 5 has a sharp by it, you will find 5's pitch in the major scale and raise it by one half step. This interval then becomes a minor 6th. For the purposes of simplicity right now, just practice finding that 5th note and raising it one half step.

In the next book I will address minor keys and move further into altered scale degrees, altered intervals and all of the characteristics of interval recognition.

9 | MUSCLE MEMORY

I've spent this entire book talking about the tools you need to understand the basics of reading music. Now it's time to put what you've learned into practice. Again, the major scale for now is going to be the foundation. Within that scale are distances from one note to another. This distance is called an interval. Over time you will be able to sing these intervals and not have to rely on the note number of the scale.

One of the ways you will be able to sing these intervals quickly is by muscle memory. There are muscles that control our vocal cords and these muscles become trained like any other muscle in the body. As we hear pitches, our vocal cords actually go into certain positions without a person making a sound. Hence we can literally become vocally tired by watching a piece of music and hearing the pitches in our head.

This is fascinating and yet necessary for us to be able to sing a note precisely on pitch. As we learn to recognize interval distances on paper, we can then join this knowledge with our muscle memory and be able to recognize and sing intervals on site.

The more you practice, the more you will be able to feel the interval of a 5th as opposed to having to count up 5 spaces or notes. This, along with hearing the interval will help you develop great proficiency in reading music.

10 | INTERVALS

So far we know that we will use the major scale with the number system to start developing our reading skills. In addition to that, it's important that you start practicing intervals by listening to them both separate and together. An **interval** is a distance between two notes. Remember earlier I stated that there are 12 notes total that we learn. Since only 7 of those occur in a scale, that leaves the other 5 notes in between which sometimes appear in the key. The intervals that make up a major scale are:

Unison or 1
Major 2nd
Major 3rd
Perfect 4th
Perfect 5th
Major 6th
Major 7th
Octave (or the repeat of notes 1 and 8, consecutively lower and higher)

The interval names for all 12 distances from 1 are as follows:

Minor 2nd
Major 2nd
Minor 3rd
Major 3rd
Perfect 4th
Tritone
Perfect 5th
Minor 6th
Major 6th
Minor 7th
Major 7th
Octave

When one of these intervals is altered (raised or lowered with a sharp or flat) then they become minor intervals or the tritone.

Don't be concerned at this point about why these interval names exist, like Tritone, or Perfect. For our purposes, we'll just memorize them and practice singing them.

Example of Major Scale Intervals

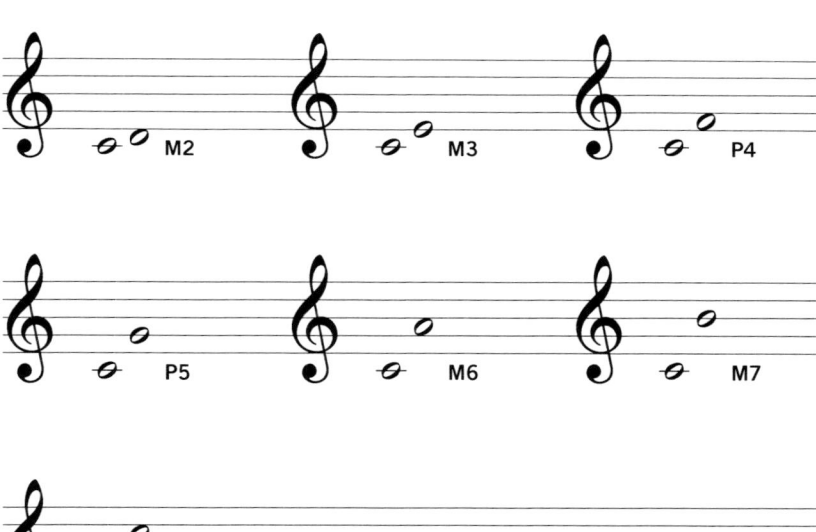

Example of Altered Intervals

Remember that if a note is raised or sharp, it is still called by a minor name. For example: The following interval is from C – G#. Technically, that is a raised 5th, but we will call it a minor 6th because we want to stay within the 12 given interval names.

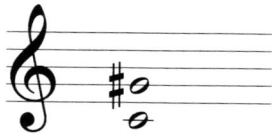

Inverted Intervals

An interval that is inverted becomes an opposite interval to complete the full scale distance. For instance, if you invert a minor 2nd, it will become a major 7th.

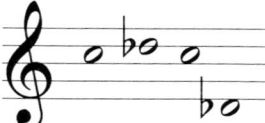

All inverted intervals change from Minor to Major and from Major to Minor. Also, the opposite number will add to equal 9 in each case.

And so on.

11 | THINGS TO THINK ABOUT

You can sing an interval (one note to another note) in several ways. Remember that with practice, muscle memory kicks in and less thinking is involved. Until you master this, there are ways to find the second note of the interval.

1. Some people are fortunate to have perfect pitch. For them, we have no sympathy. :)

2. Memorize what the different intervals sound like. Listen for characteristics of intervals. For instance, when you hear a tritone interval, it may sound dissonant to you or remind you of an ambulance siren in Europe. A major 2nd interval may remind you of the song "Chopsticks" which we all learn as kids.

3. Count up from 1 in a scale until you get to the second note.

4. Get in small groups and drill each other. It's more fun that way and more challenging to keep up with those faster and more accurate than you.

Being a teacher for so long, I've learned which roadblocks make singers miss certain intervals and why. Below are some of my observations.

When females hear intervals out of their range, they tend to invert the interval in their head and hear it incorrectly. For example, a 4th out of a female's range will be heard as a 5th.

When males hear intervals out of their range, they tend to invert the interval in their head and hear it incorrectly as well. For example, a minor 3rd out of a male's range will be heard as a major 6th.

Singing intervals downward tends to be harder for this reason. When you sing up an interval of a 5th, you are also singing to the 5th note of the scale or key. When you sing down an interval or distance of a 5th you are singing to the 4th note of the scale or key. Always remember, when you invert an interval, the addition of the inverted interval will equal 9 and cause the major to sound minor and minor to sound major. For example, a major 6th when inverted becomes a minor 3rd.

When intervals are sung ascending or descending, they tend to be heard differently depending on the direction of which they are sung. For instance, when asked to sing a minor interval descending, the interval will tend to sound major and vice versa.

12 | IN CLOSING

Remember that we combine all of our tools to help in the sight-reading process. If you read only by interval, meaning from one note to another, and you make one mistake, the rest of the notes will be incorrect. If you read only by number in relation to key center, and somehow forget where the 1's pitch was, then you will also be singing incorrectly. Once you learn to put these two methods together, you are on your way to sightreading.

When studying this material, it is best to work with an instructor or friend. This way you are able to check yourself to see if you are doing it correctly.

I hope that you now have at least a basic understanding of how all of this works. Like I mentioned in the beginning, processing speed is what takes time. I encourage everyone to get a copy of the book called *Melodia: A Course in Sight-Singing*, by Samuel Cole and Leo Lewis. It is a great practice tool for learning to read music and has every possible key signature, time signature and rhythm imaginable. If you can read that book from beginning to end, then you can read anything.

Until next time, practice, practice, practice....

NOTES

NOTES